I Will
Always
Remember
You

I Will Always Remember You

A collection of poems
Edited by Susan Polis Schutz

Blue Mountain Press ™

Boulder, Colorado

Library of Congress Number: 83-073534
ISBN: 0-88396-201-2

The following works have previously appeared in Blue Mountain Arts publications:

"It isn't always easy," by Laine Parsons. Copyright © Blue Mountain Arts, Inc., 1980. "You are always my friend," by Susan Polis Schutz. Copyright © Stephen Schutz and Susan Polis Schutz, 1982. "I think about you so much" and "I know that lately," by Susan Polis Schutz. Copyright © Stephen Schutz and Susan Polis Schutz, 1983. "I know you're not expecting this," by Jamie Delere; "Remember that eventually," by Laine Parsons; "Good-bye is such," by Edmund O'Neill; "One More Time" and "When something is over," by Lindsay Newman; "As We Go Our Separate Ways," "Think about me sometimes" and "I feel a little sad today," by Andrew Tawney. Copyright © Blue Mountain Arts, Inc., 1983. All rights reserved.

Thanks to the Blue Mountain Arts creative staff.

ACKNOWLEDGMENTS appear on page 62.

Manufactured in the United States of America
First Printing: January, 1984

Blue Mountain Press INC.

P.O. Box 4549, Boulder, Colorado 80306

CONTENTS

How do you say good-bye
to someone you shared
a love with . . .

to someone who brought
so much joy
and fulfillment . . .

How do you say good-bye
and let go
of that which
you once held. . .
to comfort and
to nourish
and to love . . .

I don't think
we can ever really
say good-bye . . .
anymore than
we could say
good-bye to our hearts.

We will survive,
we will feel love again, but
we will never forget
each other.

— Rick Norman

Sometimes I'm surprised
To find how much
You're still with me,
How easily my mind finds you
In searching for a place to rest.
It seems that somewhere
In the months and miles
Between us,
The thought of you
Should have faded . . .
But no,
At the slightest reason —
Indeed,
For no reason at all —
I think of you.

— Patricia D. Fosket

Today I was reminded
    of you . . .
taken back to a special
    place in time . . .
And as I thought of you,
a certain sort of sadness
    filled my heart . . .
Even though the memories
    we have are beautiful
and thinking back on them
    fills my heart with joy,
my eyes also swell with tears
because we are so far apart,
    and I miss you very much.

— Debbie Avery

As We Go Our Separate Ways

I don't know what to say . . .
in some ways our time together
    seems so short;
in other ways,
    there was time enough
        to get to know each other
    and time to enjoy a relationship.
But there was also time . . .
    time enough to change.

Sometimes . . . whether we
    like it or not,
people change and
    circumstances change . . .

These are the things
    that we can't do anything about.
But . . . just as the
    seasons of life change
and transcend into something
    equally as nice,
so, too, do I want
    the love we had
        to become
            the friendship
                we'll never lose.

— Andrew Tawney

I think about you so much
I wonder if you are having fun
I wonder if you are happy
I wonder if you are feeling well
Though we don't see each other
　　very often
you are with me
in my thoughts

— Susan Polis Schutz

Love,
though we have mutually agreed
that going our separate ways
is best for both of us
at this time in our lives
I hope you believe
that wherever my road takes me
I will still love you
And that in my life without you
I will always think of you
and pray for your happiness.

— Lois Reiko Shikuma

One More Time . . .

I'd really like to see you
if only for one more time . . .
Because I want each of us
to carry in our minds
nothing but good thoughts
    and fond memories
of the other
I want the times we had
    together
to remain an important part
    of our lives
And mostly, I want us to
    always be friends

I want to see you again . . .
just to see your smile
    and hear your voice
if only for one more time . . .
I want to remember you as a
    person I loved;
I want to know that you're
    still my friend.

— Lindsay Newman

I'm sorry I've hurt you.
Love is not always
full of joy.
Sometimes there is pain,
such as having to say good-bye
to someone you have loved;
someone you have laughed
and cried with;
who shared the bad time
as well as the good;
someone who listened to
your hopes and dreams,
cared about your needs and fears;
someone who was there when
no one else was,
and made your life a
better place to be
because of knowing them . . .

It's so hard to let go
of the comfortable past.
But for us to grow and be happy,
   we must.
What we had was good for us,
   when it was.
So for the sake of what
we meant to each other,
and for the memories that will
always live in our hearts,
let's say good-bye
while there is still a chance
   for us to be friends.

— Nancye Sims

Maybe once again . . .

Thank you
for all the times you held me
for all the dreams you let me dream
and for making it feel so right.
And maybe . . .
    if it really is right,
our two paths will once again
    turn into one.

— Cindy Kirkendall

Thank you
   for the times alone
   and the quietness
      of your touch
for the times we've talked
   and the honesty
      of your thoughts
for the times in the afternoon
   when we watched
      the world together

      Thank you
         for letting me
         love you.

            — Jennifer Sue Oatey

It isn't always easy . . .
   this thing called life
Plans don't always work out
   the way they're supposed to
   and misfortune sometimes
   clouds the horizon
But . . . no matter how lonely
   the morning sun becomes
   we always have to remember that
It's up to us —
   we're the ones
   that have to push
   the clouds away

— Laine Parsons

Good-bye is such a difficult word . . .
when someone is loved deeply
and sincerely, it's only natural
to always want them near —
to dream about the future together,
to share the everyday events,
to cherish, strengthen and love.

And yet, dreams don't always work out,
and good-byes, no matter how painful,
are sometimes necessary. But the love
once shared is never forgotten;
and once cherished,
a person lives forever . . .
within our hearts.

— Edmund O'Neill

It is time for us to say,
    "Good-bye . . ."
Time for our lives to take
    another path . . .
to discover new worlds.

We shared a lot of times
    together,
and we've done a lot of things.
I like to think that what we've
    learned from each other
has helped to shape us into
    better people . . .

But now, it's time to say
  "Good-bye . . ."
though not forever —
Our paths will cross again
  another day.

So, have no tears,
just think of what we had
  and smile
because everything about our
friendship is good.

And until another day . . .
  "Good-bye, my friend."

— Ann Decker

I hope that you find . . .
   the rainbow you are searching
      for,
   the happiness and joy that
      you deserve,
   the comfort of having someone
      to travel through life with,
   friends who will always care.
I hope that you live the rest
   of your life in love
      and harmony.

— Donna Wayland

One day
at a time —
this is enough.
Do not look back
and grieve over
    the past,
for it is gone;
and do not be troubled
about the future,
for it has not yet come.
Live in the present,
and make it so beautiful
that it will be worth
    remembering.

— Ida Scott Taylor

I know that lately you
have been having problems
and I just want you to know
that you can rely on me
   for anything
you might need
But more important
keep in mind at all times
that you are very capable
of dealing with any complications
that life has to offer
So
do whatever you must
feel whatever you must
and keep in mind at all times
that we all
grow wiser and
become more sensitive and
are able to enjoy life more
after we go through
hard times

— Susan Polis Schutz

If I could reach inside myself
and give to you the faith
I have in your strengths,
No mountain would be too high
for you to climb,
No detour would be able to keep
you from your goal,
Each morning would bring new hope
for yesterday's hurts.
If you had my belief in yourself,
you would know
Tomorrow is the keeper
of all your dreams.

— Vicki M. Young

Good-bye . . .

I know you'll do fine
We had everything going,
    except enough time
And we never were together
    long enough to know
How we might have made it
    or where we could go

And there's nothing else,
    Honey, that I can do
Except to tell you I once
    loved you
And we'll make better friends
    than lovers
And in trusting me,
    you might trust another . . .
So Good-bye, Babe . . .
                Good-bye.

— Kate Wolf

Never shall I forget
the days which I spent
with you . . .
Continue to be my friend,
as you will always
find me yours.

— Ludwig van Beethoven

remember
that eventually you're going to
adjust to the changes life brings your way,
and you'll realize that
it's okay to love again and laugh again,
and it's okay to get to the point where
the life you live
is full and satisfying and good to you . . .
and it will be that way
because you made it that way.

— Laine Parsons

Friend . . .
Who you are and what you
                mean to me
are expressions of what
                life means to me.
I am thankful that in this time
                our paths merge.
Only the future knows
how long we will travel the same ways,
certain only that our lives will be changed
because of our common experiences.
Let's enjoy the walk together
                and celebrate
the person each of us brings to the journey
and the friends we are becoming
along the way.

— Nancy Ferrell

You are always
    my friend
when I am happy
or when I am sad
when I am all alone
or when I am with people
You are always my friend
if I see you today
or if I see you
    a year from now
if I talk to you today
or if I talk to you
    a year from now
You are always my friend
    and though through the years
we will change
it doesn't matter what I do
or it doesn't matter what you do
Throughout our lifetime
you are always my friend

— Susan Polis Schutz

Call me someday.
When I least expect it — call me.
Call and tell me the very best
of news —
tell me you're really happy —
tell me you're feeling good,
working well,
playing hard,
doing just great, thank you.
Just call someday, and let me know
you're alive and well
and happy.

— Michael J. Mulvena

Friends sometimes
        grow apart
for the least significant
        of reasons . . .
They become busy or a new facet
        is added to their lives
and the friendship is forgotten.
I pray that this is not
        happening to us
because our friendship is
        important to me
and such a growing part of my life.
I love you and need your friendship,
as I hope that you still need mine.

— Christine Lynn Moore

I wish you well. . .

When voices fill my dream-filled
    mind, and in my thoughts,
it's you I find . . . I wish you well.

When memories of our times
    together bring a smile for the
days we both still treasure . . .
                    I wish you well.

When music plays and the words
    are true, and I think of melodies
shared with you . . . I wish you well.

When holidays spark loneliness
    of being apart, and the feelings
swell within my heart . . . I wish you well.

When photo albums show loved ones
    we both knew, and I recall the
days shared with you . . . I wish you well.

Always know that my love is near,
    and also know that . . . I wish you well.

— Edith Schaffer Lederberg

Please try to understand . . .

I need space and time
    to sort out my feelings.
I don't mean to be selfish;
I'm not only thinking of
    myself.
I do have your best interests
    in mind.
I care about you, and I don't
    want to see you hurt,
but before I can know what
    is best for us . . .
I must find out what is best
    for me.
Just give me a chance to
    find myself.
In doing this, I will respect
    you and care for you
so much more.

— Kelly Corinne Smith

We come together
for brief, beautiful
moments in time
And for awhile,
time stands still
And all we know is
the boundlessness
of our love

But then, as always,
time and the world
come crashing into
our universe
once again
And we must leave
each other
Yet, we are each
more alive
more nourished . . .

more loved
than before
And we are both grateful

For we know that
we have a secret
treasure that only
a few may ever know

And we are content
in the knowledge that
we will continue
to grow, to share,
to dream, to love
together
in other beautiful
moments to come
        . . . in time

— Jane Caldwell

We knew in the beginning
        that it couldn't last
We knew it was
        never meant to be
But while it lasted,
        it was beautiful,
And all the emptiness
        and longing I feel
        now . . .
Was worth loving you,
        even for just
        a little while.

— Jo A. Glatz

When something is over . . .

Accept that it is over
Don't try to keep living in
   the past,
and don't spend your life
   waiting for it to return
Just be glad for the good
   times you had
and for the memories you
   still keep
Then get on with your life . . .
   it's too valuable
to be spent on anything else
   but happiness and well-being.

— Lindsay Newman

There are times in every life
when we feel hurt or alone . . .
But I believe that these times
when we feel lost
and all around us seems
        to be falling apart
    are really bridges of growth.
We struggle and try to recapture
    the security of what was,
        but almost in spite of ourselves
we emerge on the other side
with a new understanding,
        a new awareness,
        a new strength.
It is almost as though
        we must go through the pain
            and the struggle
                in order to grow
and reach new heights.

— Sue Mitchell

I know you're not
   expecting this . . .
but it's something
I've been wanting to say for so long.

It has been bothering me lately when,
thinking back, I can recall
so many times when I was
so involved with me
that I didn't pay as much
attention to you
or talk about things with you
as I should have . . .
and as you so surely deserved.

It's not that I didn't want to . . .
it's just that I sometimes get
   confused about what's going on,
and the more confused I get,
the more silent I get
and the more I retreat within
   to feel safe and secure . . .
For any time I was ever
inconsiderate to you,
   or too quiet or too private,
I hope you'll forgive me.

— Jamie Delere

You're still on my mind . . .

After all is said and done
A few things lost, a few things
    won,
I can say I've had a full and a
    happy life.
But in the quiet of the night
When I turn out the light
I'm amazed to find that you're
    still on my mind . . .

I could be talking with my friends
Or out walking when day ends
Or just doing all the things that
    fill my time.
But at the closing of the day
When my troubles fade away
I'm amazed to find that you're
    still on my mind . . .

— Kate Wolf

I know that you are feeling
        disillusioned now,
but life has a way of balancing
        the sorrow with the joy,
        the disappointment with the
            hope,
        the emptiness with the meaning.

Someday, my friend, you will
        look back on this time
in your life
as a period of learning, growing
    and discovering
your own strength.

Until the sunshine comes back
    into your life,
remember . . .
    I am your friend,
and know . . .
    I really do care.

                    — Paula Finn

"Special" is a word
that is used to describe
something one-of-a-kind
like a hug
or a sunset
or a person who spreads love
with a smile or kind gesture.
"Special" describes people
who act from the heart
and keep in mind the hearts of others.
"Special" applies to something
that is admired and precious
and which can never be replaced.
"Special" is the word that best
describes you.

— Teri Fernandez

I feel a little sad today,
and I don't know why . . .
maybe it's because
I'm right here,
and you seem so far away.
I can't just call you up
like I used to, and ask you to come over;
I can't just drop in and say "hello" . . .

I guess what I'm saying
is that
I miss you.
I really do!
And it isn't easy,
    but it is kind of nice . . .
thinking that you
might be missing me, too.

— Andrew Tawney

When things don't work out
    with a relationship . . .
you feel lost, a little empty
        sad and angry.
You need to sit back
and sort out your feelings
        and thoughts,
remembering that
if it was meant to be,
it will return.
But if not . . . then it is best
    that it's gone.
You will always learn
    and you will continue to grow
        from the experience.

— Barbara Gladys

Think about me sometimes . . . okay?
Even though we're not together
        the way we used to be,
it still seems so natural
        and so easy to think of you
and all the good times we shared.

Any hard times we had
seem to fade away so quietly,
but the memories of all the
        smiles and special times
    will stay with us
    and never disappear.

Guess I just wanted
to say "hello . . ."
and tell you that
I have one wish
that I wish you'd grant me —
for old-times' sake, today:
        just that I hope you'll
            think about me
                sometimes . . . okay?

— Andrew Tawney

ACKNOWLEDGMENTS

We gratefully acknowledge the permission granted by the following authors, publishers and authors' representatives to reprint poems and excerpts from their publications.

Rick Norman for "How do you say good-bye," by Rick Norman. Copyright © Rick Norman, 1982. All rights reserved. Reprinted by permission.

Patricia D. Fosket for "Sometimes I'm surprised," by Patricia D. Fosket. Copyright © Patricia D. Fosket, 1982. All rights reserved. Reprinted by permission.

Debbie Avery for "Today I was reminded of you," by Debbie Avery. Copyright © Debbie Avery, 1983. All rights reserved. Reprinted by permission.

Lois Reiko Shikuma for "Love, though we have," by Lois Reiko Shikuma. Copyright © Lois Reiko Shikuma, 1984. All rights reserved. Reprinted by permission.

Nancye Sims for "I'm sorry I've hurt you," by Nancye Sims. Copyright © Nancye Sims, 1984. All rights reserved. Reprinted by permission.

Cindy Kirkendall for "Maybe once again . . . ," by Cindy Kirkendall. Copyright © Cindy Kirkendall, 1983. All rights reserved. Reprinted by permission.

Jennifer Sue Oatey for "Thank you for the times," by Jennifer Sue Oatey. Copyright © Jennifer Sue Oatey, 1981. All rights reserved. Reprinted by permission.

Ann Decker for "It is time for us," by Ann Decker. Copyright © Ann Decker, 1984. All rights reserved. Reprinted by permission.

Donna Wayland for "I hope that you find . . . ," by Donna Wayland. Copyright © Donna Wayland, 1984. All rights reserved. Reprinted by permission.

Vicki M. Young for "If I could reach inside," by Vicki M. Young. Copyright © Vicki M. Young, 1984. All rights reserved. Reprinted by permission.

Kate Wolf for "I know you'll do fine," from the song GOODBYE, BABE, by Kate Wolf. Copyright © 1975 Another Sundown Publishing. And for "After all is said and done," from the song AMAZED TO FIND, by Kate Wolf. Copyright © 1977 Another Sundown Publishing. All rights reserved. Reprinted by permission.

Nancy Ferrell for "Friend . . . Who you are," by Nancy Ferrell. Copyright © Nancy Ferrell, 1981. All rights reserved. Reprinted by permission.